Matthew 7:3-5 New International Version (NIV) 3

"Why do you look at the speck of sawdust in your brother's eye and pay no attention to the plank in your own eye? 4 How can you say to your brother, 'Let me take the speck out of your eye,' when all the time there is a plank in your own eye? 5 You hypocrite, first take the plank out of your own eye, and then you will see clearly to remove the speck from your brother's eye.

Fooled
No More

A two year journal through chronic pain and opioids that turned into a 31-question journey toward truth. An introspective guide into the truth from within. Truth showed me that I had to become who I am not in order to become who I am destined to be. I have the power to change the trajectory of my entire life, every second, by being healthy, active, and truthful.

SASHA DREAMS

FOOLED NO MORE

Copyright © 2018 by I Dream Business, LLC

For my throne,

Genesis 11:6 King James Version (KJV)

6 And the Lord said, Behold, the people is one, and they have all one language; and this they begin to do: and now nothing will be restrained from them, which they have imagined.

#BeRooted.live

DEDICATION

This book, like the first and every book to follow, is dedicated to my ancestors. Thank you for continuing to come to me in my dreams and reminding me of my worth. I honor you.

From my soul to yours.

Full transparency: I KNOW NOTHING

"You cannot take responsibility for how well another accepts your truth; you can only ensure how well it is communicated. And by how well, I don't mean merely how clearly; I mean how lovingly, how compassionately, how sensitively, how courageously, and how completely. This leaves no room for half truths, the 'brutal truth,' or even the 'plain truth.' It does mean the truth, the whole truth, and nothing but the truth, so help you God."

– Conversations With God

Hello World,

When it comes to telling the truth, there's only a certain percentage we all are willing to tell. First of all, the truth according to who? According to who or whom, the who, what, where, when, and why? It is also hard to tell the truth due to fear. Sometimes, getting to the root of the truth seems impossible. I agree with you. I'm here to challenge us to pull the root together and maybe, just maybe, we can find those roots and truths, together.

Lies can take a lifetime to get to the root of, depending on how long the lie has had time to cultivate. I know. I've been lied to. I lied, and I may lie again. The goal is for me to stay conscious and not consciously cause any more pain to myself or others. Doing so, will comfort and allow me to be comforted. Grow with me as God (love) helps me realize the courage I need to get to the root of all my problems is already within me. Understanding that love is allowing me to share my experiences, knowing that when we are consciously united, we are powerful beyond measure.

Let's grow!

THE POWER OF NOW

A beggar had been sitting by the side of a road for over thirty years. One day a stranger walked by. "Spare some change?" mumbled the beggar, mechanically holding out his old baseball cap.

"I have nothing to give you," said the stranger. Then he asked, "What's that you are sitting on?"

"Nothing," replied the beggar. "Just an old box. I have been sitting on it for as long as I can remember."

"Ever looked inside?" asked the stranger.

"No," said the beggar. "What's the point? There's nothing in there."

"Have a look inside," insisted the stranger.

The beggar managed to pry open the lid. With astonishment, disbelief, and elation, he saw that the box was filled with gold.

I am that stranger who has nothing to give you and who is telling you to look inside. Not inside any box, as in the parable, but somewhere even closer: inside yourself. "But I am not a beggar," I can hear you say. Those who have not found their true wealth, which is the radiant joy of Being and the deep, unshakable peace that comes with it, are beggars, even if they have great material wealth. They are looking outside for scraps of pleasure or fulfillment, for validation, security, or love, while they have a treasure within that not only includes all those things but is infinitely greater than anything the world can offer.

Are you brave enough to open the box? If not, put this book away and come back when you are ready. I admit, I am still a beggar. I beg my friends and family to believe in the visions I see of the future. I beg people to listen, invest, comment, approve, and validate. I beg. It was not until I opened the box that I became aware of my begging. I went inside of myself and I became conscious. Consciously aware of my actions, and that awareness was the first step into change. Truth revealed itself and helped me understand that My destiny was waiting for me to believe in me. I believed the three-letter lie in the seven-letter word. BE LIE VE. I almost let the little lie prevent me from reaching my destiny. I say with the strongest affirmation I can muster, I humble the me in me and rebuke the lie in believe! No one will keep me from my destiny. Including me.

For those of you who are ready, don't worry, you won't have to go in alone. I will be with you. A constant friend. I will share some of my intimate journal entries. Written while, unbeknownst to me, I was getting in touch with me. I had to learn how to be honest with myself. I also had to accept that my problems do not define me. I had to be completely stripped of all the things I thought were true to get to the truth. I had to get to the point where love would ask me the ultimate question, "Who are you?" The answer took me years to find out. Please do not become frustrated if within 31 questions, you do not have a clear and concise answer. This question will be asked in many different forms throughout this journey. I am not acting as a navigator. I am not a doctor of any kind. I am only sharing with you the questions and directions my soul asked and instructed me. Sometimes, I will share with you my answers. Only to show you how far gone the pain and my circumstances had taken me and how far I've returned. If you're on this journey, this is not about me. This is for you. Please take your time on this journey.

Although this is a 31 question journal, it does not need to be completed within 31 days. Go at your own pace. There will be 3 questions every day. One from my soul, one from my mother (love). She called me all throughout my journey and asked, "How are you today?" Basic question, but it meant the world because she truly wanted to know. Not the generic response we give automatically. Truly, from your soul, How are you today? Finally, your pain level for the day. A great tool to reference for your pain journey.

Please also understand that these questions, answered honestly, may tear open some wounds that you thought were healed. Be encouraged. I faced many phantoms from my past. I am learning that they can not withstand truth. Darkness cannot survive in the light. Light shined on darkness creates light.

I am forgiving myself for many sins. I forgave others that I perceived as sinning against me. To all the people I have hurt, knowingly and unknowingly, I beg your forgiveness. I'm learning that I can choose love. In every situation. No matter how complicated or challenging, I choose love. Love has no opposite. Love is action. Let's go in the name of love. Healing of your mind, body, and soul will be the goal towards peace, more love, and happiness. Follow your soul.

CONTACTS

If at any time you feel uncomfortable about your thoughts, please contact the resources and/or your doctor.

Medical

www.justanswer.com/Medical

Crisis

www.crisistextline.org

Suicide

www.d2lrevolution.com/no-suicide-zone

Addiction

www.addictionrecoverynow.net/Opiate_Detox

https://www.drugrehab.com

Prayer

www.crossroads.ca/247prayer

What do you hope to get out of this journey?

#1 Date: _____

Honestly, who are you?

Research suggests that it takes 21 days for a habit to form. Daily, I lied to myself. I told myself that my physical pain and life circumstances were greater than my ability to write. I believed the lie and became a writer who did not write. An inventor that did not invent. "I'm just not good enough." I said that for at least two years. Well, that's the habit I formed. It wasn't until I walked past a mirror one day and got a glimpse of the woman I used to be. There she was, standing there in all her glory. For just one second, I recognized her. For just one second, I saw her for who she really was. Before the surgery, before the feelings of inadequacies controlled me. I appreciated that moment and decided to spend the next days of my life trying my hardest to get her back.

Starting anything new can be challenging, but the reward can be unimaginable. I invite you to go to the mirror. Any mirror. Wash your face, take off any jewelry, head scarves or hats or hair pieces. Strip yourself down to your bare self.

Honestly, who are you?

_____

_____

_____

_____

_____

_____

_____

_____

_____

_____

_____

_____

_____

_____

_____

_____

_____

_____

_____

_____

_____

_____

Date: _____

Pain Level?

No pain   0,   1,   2,   3,   4,   5,   6,   7,   8,   9,   10   Extreme
pain

How are you today? Love wants to know.

_____

_____

_____

_____

_____

_____

_____

_____

_____

_____

_____

_____

_____

_____

_____

#2 Date: _____

How do you forgive?

Over the span of my life, I have had to forgive myself and others for various situations. It was not until I thought about what forgiveness meant to me that I realized that my forgiveness needed a lot more forgiveness. The day I sought the true definition of forgiveness, the universe put on my mind my old track partner from high school. Im talking seventeen years ago high school friend from another state. For the strangest reason, I kept bumping into her. We would stop, hug, chat a little bit about life currently, and keep it moving. When I sought the definition of forgiveness, love told me to pass the baton.

Pass the baton? It all became so clear. Forgiveness is just like passing the baton in track and field. My old friend from school and I ran the 4X100 and 4X200 together. We always ran the last two legs. Either she ran anchor or I did, depending on the mood of the coach. I particularly liked running third; speeding and leaning around the track, with your spikes in the asphalt and the wind against your face, your classmates screaming for you in encouragement and holding on to the baton as if my life depended on it, is one of the most exhilarating experiences of my life thus far. When handing the baton, you reach out with all your strength, holding on for dear life and unwilling to let go until until you are sure your teammate has the baton. Anyway, I envisioned forgiving myself for all of the things I was holding a grudge against myself for. All the lies I believed. I imagined two of me, I saw myself hand my new self, my self who is set free from the sins of the past, the self who is made whole because I forgive her. Not that I've forgotten anything. I am set free from the guilt, the hurt, and the shame. I see the old me, I do not tear her down anymore. She did what she did. I must be willing to be proud of her for getting me to this point. Now pass the baton confidently and be willing to change.

How do you forgive?

_____
_____
_____
_____
_____
_____
_____

_____

_____

Date: _____

Pain Level?

No pain   0,   1,   2,   3,   4,   5,   6,   7,   8,   9,   10   Extreme pain

How are you today? Love wants to know.

_____

_____

_____

_____

_____

_____

_____

_____

_____

_____

_____

_____

_____

#3 Date: _____

Rock bottom?

For some reason I had to be brought down low in order to abound. I had to be terminated, denied, isolated, broken down physically and mentally, left alone, abandoned and afraid, rightfully confused, discouraged, and drugged in order to get to this moment.

What does rock bottom look like for you?

_____

_____

_____

_____

_____

_____

_____

_____

_____

_____

_____

_____

_____

Date: _____

Pain Level?

No pain 0, 1, 2, 3, 4, 5, 6, 7, 8, 9, 10 Extreme pain

How are you today? Love wants to know.

_____

_____

_____

_____

_____

_____

_____

_____

_____

_____

_____

_____

_____

_____

_____

#4 Date: _____

What is the universe saying to you?

12/2/2017 – I am broken yet so thankful. The universe has clearly told me."You are not alone." I've been awake all night, feeling completely alone. Pain on 10. I reached out to family for a solution to distract me from the pain. A solution that involved me leaving the house so that I wouldn't just take more drugs. Family was busy. I looked on Meetup.com for purpose. I was led to "Yana Sisterhood" that had a Meetup scheduled for that same day. A woman posted that she could not attend and was offering her prepaid ticket. Where? A tea at a hotel! Dear God, I love you and I know I am not living up to your expectations. I am the worse. Wallowing in pain. Wanting the world, but what am I prepared to contribute?"

I went looking for purpose and purpose revealed itself. It was not clear to me that day that I would create another Meetup of my own (I created one in 2015 for authors), but the seed was planted. Even though my pain was great and the excuses roared, I was willing. I pushed past the pain and was able to have an amazing time with a group of amazing women. Thank you to the woman who gave the universe her ticket. You helped save my life.

What is the universe saying to you?

Date: _____

Pain Level?

No pain   0,   1,   2,   3,   4,   5,   6,   7,   8,   9,   10   Extreme pain

How are you today? Love wants to know.

_____

_____

_____

_____

_____

_____

_____

_____

_____

_____

_____

_____

_____

_____

_____

_____

_____

_____

_____

_____

#5 Date: _____

What is your purpose?

1/15/18 – Give birth to what is in you. My uterus was taken, but I'm still pregnant with dreams. Begging God to stop the pain. All the while, He is begging me to push. Push past the pain and trust Him. Put pen to paper and give the world what He has given me. Until I give birth to His Word, I will live captive. Captivated by my mind. A constant tormentor. A mind that hates me. A mind that will not forgive me. A mind that doesn't even want me to write these words. My chest tightens. Air hides. I am temporarily distracted by nothing. The mind's tricks are limitless. Still. I push. Push past the denial letter. Push past the chronic pain. Push past the side effects. Push past the declination of my credit score. Push past the cloud that's engulfed my being and push.

Here I am Lord. Lying prone. In need of prayer and support. A midwife will do.

Although, I will go alone. I push. Alas, your humble servant, I say yes to your will.

Yes, I see the holes in my baby's socks. Yet, I stay still. Motionless. Unwilling to trust your Word. Denying my soul what it craves. Push. I hear the wrestling of the dying leaves in fall scratch against the depleted land. Turn my head toward You I feel. Give in.

I will no longer allow my mind to control me. I will listen to the silence from within. Now. I have birthed my purpose.

This is, fill in the blank, what is your purpose?

_____

_____

_____

_____

_____

_____

_____

_____

_____

_____

_____

_____

_____

_____

_____

_____

Date: _____

Pain Level?

No pain   0,   1,   2,   3,   4,   5,   6,   7,   8,   9,   10   Extreme pain

How are you today? Love wants to know.

_____

_____

_____

_____

_____

_____

_____

_____

_____

_____

_____

_____

_____

_____

_____

_____

_____

_____

#6 Date: _____

Side Effects: Drugs and lies can keep you stuck in dysfunction.

What are the side effects of your actions?

_____

_____

_____

_____

_____

_____

_____

_____

_____

_____

_____

_____

_____

_____

_____

_____

Date: _____

Pain Level?

No pain 0, 1, 2, 3, 4, 5, 6, 7, 8, 9, 10 Extreme pain

How are you today? Love wants to know.

_____

_____

_____

_____

_____

_____

_____

_____

_____

_____

_____

_____

_____

_____

_____

_____

_____

#7 Date: _____

Where is your faith?

Turning Pages is the name of my book club. We have been together for a lifetime now. One particular meeting, I was well into the wine and boy, way I was whining. I was down on my girlfriends carpet, careful not to spill a sip of wine, moaning and groaning about how I had no idea how my life was going to "work out." One of my dear friends slides in real close to me. Really in my face, and asks, "Where is your faith?" The fire in her words felt like a rake with the drag of a grape vine across the face. Faith is defined in the bible as hope in the seen and the unseen. And faith without work is dead.

Where is your faith?

_____

_____

_____

43

_____

_____

_____

_____

_____

Date: _____

Pain Level?

No pain   0,   1,   2,   3,   4,   5,   6,   7,   8,   9,   10   Extreme pain

How are you today? Love wants to know.

_____

_____

_____

_____

_____

_____

_____

_____

_____

_____

_____

_____

_____

_____

_____

_____

_____

_____

#8 Date: _____

Who are you blaming?

Taking responsibility for the role I play in any situation has been challenging to face. It's much easier to blame others.It's much easier to play the victim rather than the villain. At this stage of my life, I have been an adult much longer than I was a child. It's time I accept my role in this. Face my mistakes, my on-purposes. Admit that I lied. Admit that I believed the lies I told. Receive forgiveness, and now it's time to pass the baton. Oftentimes, there is another person to blame. Oftentimes, there is an evil villain. In those instances, its best to forgive the pain they caused and either report them to authorities, or pass them a new baton if your spirit believes they will not harm you again.

Who are you blaming?

46

_____

_____

_____

_____

_____

_____

Date: _____

Pain Level?

No pain   0,   1,   2,   3,   4,   5,   6,   7,   8,   9,   10   Extreme pain

How are you today? Love wants to know.

_____

_____

_____

_____

_____

_____

_____

_____

_____

_____

_____

_____

_____

_____

_____

_____

_____

 # 9 Date: _____

Giving without expecting anything in return. How do you give?

It has been very frustrating for me to share "what's on my mind" on facebook or send out a tweet or text. The reason it's frustrating for me is because I am begging for approval. I am anxious to hear a comment or receive a like. A response that says my thoughts are good enough. Anxious to see if someone new may like or retweet my "profound" thoughts. I am left exasperated. "What's on my mind" apparently isn't as "profound" as I may have thought because so-and-so did not respond. I see that she or he liked someone else's comment, so they are obviously aware that I had something "profound" to say. The agony caused me not to say anything. I have recently learned that I must give and share without any

49

expectation that anyone is going to like, comment, or share. It's not about receiving. It's about giving. It feels so good to share. My soul craves it. Whether it's "right" or "wrong." My intention is love. Nina Simone sings, "I'm just a soul whose intentions are good, oh, Lord, please don't let me be misunderstood." Thank you to Chells who made a song from his soul for me in my first book. ItTakesAFool.com.

How do you give?

_____

_____

_____

_____

_____

_____

_____

_____

_____

_____

_____

_____

_____

_____

_____

_____

_____

_____

_____

_____

Date: _____

Pain Level?

No pain   0,   1,   2,   3,   4,   5,   6,   7,   8,   9,   10   Extreme pain

How are you today? Love wants to know.

_____

_____

_____

_____

_____

_____

_____

_____

_____

_____

_____

_____

_____

_____

_____

_____

_____

_____

_____

#10 Date: _____

Truth is in the silence. What are your loved ones saying to you in their silence?

About twenty years ago, I first read Iyanla V Yesterday, I cried. There's a scene in that book that is forever etched into my mind. Iyanla's uncle sexually assaults her in the home she shared her her aunt and uncle. The scene is painted so vividly with every sense, sight, smell, sound and touch. You can feel and smell the pain in her words. Iyanla talks about waiting for her aunt to come home because she just knew her aunt was going to destroy the uncle. Her aunt comes home. Even though their normally impeccably clean home appears as if robbers had come in with the overturned furniture and trash thrown, all evidence from the assault, her aunt is silent. Iyanla cries secretly for the screams and shouts, the bag packing of the uncle the police being phoned. Something. But there was only silence.

Silence may be hard to accept. I have had to accept the silence of loved ones. I am currently accepting the silence of loved ones. I now know to pay close attention to all of what people are not saying. A lot of times, it says more than what they are saying.

What are your loved ones saying to you in their silence?

"You can accept or reject the way you are treated by other people, but until you heal the wounds of your past, you will continue to bleed. You can bandage the bleeding with food, with alcohol, with drugs, with work, with cigarettes, with sex, but eventually, it will all ooze through and stain your life. You must find the strength to open the wounds, stick your hands inside, pull out the core of the pain that is holding you in your past, the memories, and make peace with them."

– Iyanla Vanzant

_____

_____

_____

_____

_____

_____

_____

_____

_____

Date: _____

Pain Level?

No pain   0,   1,   2,   3,   4,   5,   6,   7,   8,   9,   10   Extreme pain

How are you today? Love wants to know.

_____

_____

_____

_____

_____

_____

_____

_____

_____

_____

_____

_____

_____

_____

_____

#11 Date: _____

What are you resisting?

Getting in touch with your purpose can be challenging. Donald Neale Walsh says, "Life begins at the end of your comfort zone." I had to get extremely uncomfortable in order to get in touch with my purpose. Even as I write these words, I am afraid. I am still wrestling. But, I come.

What are you resisting?

_____

_____

_____

_____

_____

_____

_____

_____

_____

_____

_____

_____

_____

Date: _____

Pain Level?

No pain 0, 1, 2, 3, 4, 5, 6, 7, 8, 9, 10 Extreme pain

How are you today? Love wants to know.

_____

_____

_____

_____

_____

_____

_____

_____

_____

_____

_____

_____

_____

_____

_____

_____

#12 Date: _____

Everything happens for a reason?

It has taking forever for me to accept that. This "everything" has proven itself to be monstrous at times. Not just in my life, but in history and the current world news. This "everything" has the power to steal, kill, and destroy. I watch helplessly as it occurs. How and why did I end up here? More importantly, what will I do next?

Does everything happen for a reason?

_____

_____

_____

_____

_____

_____

_____

_____

_____

_____

_____

_____

Date: _____

Pain Level?

No pain   0,   1,   2,   3,   4,   5,   6,   7,   8,   9,   10   Extreme
pain

How are you today? Love wants to know.

_____

_____

_____

_____

_____

_____

_____

_____

_____

_____

_____

_____

_____

_____

#13 Date: _____

Are you present? You have to have both feet together in the now.

Double Dutch. I was never any good at the game double dutch. It never seemed like there was enough time to jump in. Sometimes, when my cousins were patient, they would let me start in the rope. They would lay down the ropes, exaggerating and slowly raising the ropes to let me get physically and mentally prepared to jump. Both feet together. None of that fancy stuff you see where people jump from side to side. Up, down. Back and forth. I'm talking real live circus acts can be performed inside of a double dutch rope. Not me, though. Both feet together, starting from inside the rope. As sad as my rhythm may be, it teaches me the lesson on presence. In order to be 100% in the now, in the here and now, I have to have both feet together. Not one foot in the past or one foot in my projected future, that does not exist. But both feet, right here, right now. Be in tune with your being. In tune with your being's pace and timing. Ask your being what all it needs and you shall receive.

Are you present?

Date: _____

Pain Level?

No pain 0, 1, 2, 3, 4, 5, 6, 7, 8, 9, 10 Extreme pain

How are you today? Love wants to know.

_____

_____

_____

_____

_____

_____

_____

_____

_____

_____

_____

_____

_____

_____

_____

_____

_____

_____

#14 Date: _____

Go inwards?

Conversations with God, Neale Donald Walsch

"If you do not go within, you go without. Put it in the first person as you repeat it, to make it more personal: If I do not go within I go without. You have been going without all your life. Yet you do not have to, and never did."

_____

_____

_____

_____

_____

_____

_____

_____

_____

_____

_____

_____

_____

_____

_____

Date: _____

Pain Level?

No pain   0,   1,   2,   3,   4,   5,   6,   7,   8,   9,   10   Extreme
pain

How are you today? Love wants to know.

_____

_____

_____

_____

_____

_____

_____

_____

_____

_____

_____

_____

_____

_____

_____

_____

#15 Date: _____

What problems are surrounding you?

"What problems can there be when love is surrounding me?" My responses were truthful. All the problems! Don't you see me in pain. Pain from my surgery. Pain from not receiving pay. Pain from the embarrassment of walking through the alley to see my boys, do a load of laundry, or to make a cup of coffee. Pain from the despair of the lack of control I felt. Pain of having to surrender to trusting my husband to be the man I pray that he is. Trusting love. It was painful. Relinquishing control is painful.

What problems are surrounding you?

_____

_____

_____

_____

_____

_____

_____

_____

_____

Date: _____

Pain Level?

No pain   0,   1,   2,   3,   4,   5,   6,   7,   8,   9,   10   Extreme
pain

How are you today? Love wants to know.

_____

_____

_____

_____

_____

_____

_____

_____

_____

_____

_____

_____

_____

#16 Date: _____

What are your dreams saying to you?

If you do not remember your dreams, you can be fairly confident that B-6 is part of the picture. B-6, by the way, is critical in converting your proteins such as tryptophan into key neurotransmitters such as serotonin. It certainly may aggravate your depression if you are low. When you wake up tomorrow morning, note whether you remember a dream. Carl Pfieffer describes in his book *Nutrition and Mental Illness.* *"The richest sources of vitamin B6 include fish, beef liver and other organ meats, potatoes and other starchy vegetables, and fruit (other than citrus). In the United States, adults obtain most of their dietary vitamin B6 from fortified cereals, beef, poultry, starchy vegetables, and some non-citrus fruits."* *[1,3,5].Mar 2, 2018*

What are your dreams saying to you?

_____

_____

_____

_____

_____

_____

_____

Date: _____

Pain Level?

No pain 0, 1, 2, 3, 4, 5, 6, 7, 8, 9, 10 Extreme pain

How are you today? Love wants to know.

_____

_____

_____

_____

_____

_____

_____

_____

_____

_____

_____

_____

_____

_____

_____

_____

#17 Date: _____

What are your insecurities?

_____

_____

_____

_____

_____

_____

_____

_____

_____

_____

_____

_____

_____

_____

_____

_____

_____

_____

_____

Date: _____

Pain Level?

No pain   0,   1,   2,   3,   4,   5,   6,   7,   8,   9,   10   Extreme
pain

How are you today? Love wants to know.

_____

_____

_____

_____

_____

_____

_____

_____

_____

_____

_____

_____

_____

_____

_____

_____

_____

#18 Date: _____

What all are you willing to change?

I thought I was building my dream house, but God was building me. I had to be willing to give up everything false to get to this moment. All I knew is that I wanted the vision. The promise within the vision pounded in sync with my heart. I had to be willing to change everything I thought I knew I loved, in order to get to what I knew I loved.

What are you willing to change?

_____

_____

_____

_____

_____

_____

_____

_____

_____

_____

_____

_____

Date: _____

Pain Level?

No pain 0, 1, 2, 3, 4, 5, 6, 7, 8, 9, 10 Extreme pain

How are you today? Love wants to know.

_____

_____

_____

_____

_____

_____

_____

_____

_____

_____

_____

_____

_____

_____

_____

_____

_____

#19 Date: _____

What are you focused on?

Brilliant minds need to focus on brilliant things.

What are you focused on?

_____

_____

_____

_____

_____

_____

_____

_____

_____

_____

_____

_____

_____

_____

_____

_____

Date: _____

Pain Level?

No pain   0,   1,   2,   3,   4,   5,   6,   7,   8,   9,   10   Extreme
pain

How are you today? Love wants to know.

_____

_____

_____

_____

_____

_____

_____

_____

_____

_____

_____

_____

_____

_____

_____

_____

_____

#20 Date: _____

"Healing tears?"

I remember the night I first thought tears were a sign of weakness. I also remember the night if I didn't have the tears, I wouldn't have had anything at all.

"Healing tears?"

_____

_____

_____

_____

_____

_____

_____

_____

_____

_____

_____

_____

_____

_____

Date: _____

Pain Level?

No pain   0,   1,   2,   3,   4,   5,   6,   7,   8,   9,   10   Extreme
pain

How are you today? Love wants to know.

_____

_____

_____

_____

_____

_____

_____

_____

_____

_____

_____

_____

_____

_____

_____

_____

_____

#21 Date: _____

Are you a victim?

11/30/17 – There's a battle going on all around us. We
used to be in one. Riding the same white horse. Now.
You've thrown me off. You pushed me while you were
looking straight ahead. No care as to where I fell. Left,
right, not a care. Where I fell, so freaking what? The horse
darkens, and you're riding alone in the wrong direction.
Maybe. You may have thought I served no purpose.
Taking up space and weighing you down while riding
behind. But you were fooled. My position is worth my
smile in gold. I'm here on the ground. Still shocked. But
no longer. I will get my bearings together. Brush off the
shame, hurt, inadequacy, and loneliness. Like every entity
that has a strong desire to exist, I rise.

Are you a victim?

_____

_____

_____

_____

_____

_____

_____

_____

Date: _____

Pain Level?

No pain   0,   1,   2,   3,   4,   5,   6,   7,   8,   9,   10   Extreme pain

How are you today? Love wants to know.

_____

_____

_____

_____

_____

_____

_____

_____

_____

_____

_____

_____

_____

_____

_____

_____

_____

_____

#22 Date: _____

How do you pray?

I am learning to hear truth through silence. Learning to speak less and listen more.

How do you pray?

_____

_____

_____

_____

_____

_____

_____

_____

_____

_____

_____

_____

_____

_____

_____

_____

Date: _____

Pain Level?

No pain 0, 1, 2, 3, 4, 5, 6, 7, 8, 9, 10 Extreme pain

How are you today? Love wants to know.

_____

_____

_____

_____

_____

_____

_____

_____

_____

_____

_____

_____

_____

_____

_____

_____

_____

#23 Date: _____

Options?

I was terminated on March 19, 2018. I was faced with two options. Get a job or create one. I chose the latter. #Iamnotmyemployeenumber.

What are your options?

_____

_____

_____

_____

_____

_____

_____

_____

_____

_____

_____

_____

_____

_____

_____

_____

Date: _____

Pain Level?

No pain 0, 1, 2, 3, 4, 5, 6, 7, 8, 9, 10 Extreme pain

How are you today? Love wants to know.

_____

_____

_____

_____

_____

_____

_____

_____

_____

_____

_____

_____

_____

_____

_____

_____

_____

#24 Date: _____

What is the solution?

If there is no solution, can you label it a problem? Name
the problem.

What is the solution?

_____

_____

_____

_____

_____

_____

_____

_____

_____

_____

_____

_____

_____

_____

_____

Date: _____

Pain Level?

No pain   0,   1,   2,   3,   4,   5,   6,   7,   8,   9,   10   Extreme
pain

How are you today? Love wants to know.

_____

_____

_____

_____

_____

_____

_____

_____

_____

_____

_____

_____

_____

_____

_____

_____

_____

_____

#25 Date: _____

Speaking it into existence?

I am healed. My mind is healed. My body is healed. I am whole.

What else can you speak into existence?

_____

_____

_____

_____

_____

_____

_____

_____

_____

_____

_____

_____

_____

_____

_____

_____

Date: _____

Pain Level?

No pain   0,   1,   2,   3,   4,   5,   6,   7,   8,   9,   10   Extreme pain

How are you today? Love wants to know.

_____

_____

_____

_____

_____

_____

_____

_____

_____

_____

_____

_____

_____

_____

_____

_____

_____

#26 Date: _____

Where is your accountability?

Life kept beating me down. Like the scene in The Incredibles where Mr. Incredible was getting beat by the robot. Stomp, stomp, stomp. The denial letters shook me to my core. Denied for disability, denied for medical retirement, denied by workmans comp for pay, denied the opportunity to pay my bills, denied. Thankfully, I was being transformed. The denials were shaking me and transforming me. Disrupting my internal processor.

Challenging me to rethink my entire life. Denied, but not destroyed.

Where is your accountability?

_____

_____

_____

_____

_____

_____

_____

_____

_____

_____

_____

_____

_____

_____

_____

_____

_____

_____

_____

_____

_____

_____

_____

_____

_____

_____

_____

_____

_____

_____

Date: _____

Pain Level?

No pain   0,   1,   2,   3,   4,   5,   6,   7,   8,   9,   10   Extreme
pain

How are you today? Love wants to know.

_____

_____

_____

_____

_____

_____

_____

_____

_____

_____

_____

_____

_____

_____

_____

_____

_____

_____

_____

#27 Date: _____

Are you worried?

I am worried. I am a worrier. I worry while I'm smiling. I worry while I'm crying. I worry while I'm up and I worry while I'm down. I'm like the Sam I Am of worry. Since I was twelve, I've been reading Matthew 6, Do Not Worry, and still I worry. I saw the lilies of the field, dressed in all their splendor, and still I worry. I said "I trust love", and

111

still I worry. Things in my life are currently more than what I deserve and still, I worry. My marriage, my parenting, my friends, my credit score, I worry. It wasn't until love showed me that love is the same love in everything. The alpha and the omega. The beginning and the end of all things. Showed me that love is capable of doing for them and everything else on my list. Love trumps it all. Love says, for me to bring all of my attention into me. Pray and release. Love is doing all for them that love is doing for me and I DO NOT need to worry. And with that, I can lay my burdens down. All of my worry is washed away. I need not to worry about a thing. I can rest confidently that the same love is doing for my list just like love is doing for me. Nothing is alright but everything is ok.

Are you worried?

_____

_____

_____

_____

_____

_____

_____

_____

_____

_____

_____

_____

_____

_____

_____

_____

_____

_____

_____

_____

_____

_____

Date: _____

Pain Level?

No pain   0,   1,   2,   3,   4,   5,   6,   7,   8,   9,   10   Extreme

pain

How are you today? Love wants to know.

_____

_____

_____

_____

_____

_____

_____

_____

_____

_____

_____

_____

_____

_____

_____

_____

_____

_____

_____

_____

#28 Date: _____

Your top five favorite contacts?

Proverbs 13:20 *"Walk with the wise and become wise, for a companion of fools suffers harm."*

Who are your top five favorite contacts?

_____

_____

_____

_____

_____

_____

_____

_____

_____

_____

_____

_____

_____

_____

Date: _____

Pain Level?

No pain   0,   1,   2,   3,   4,   5,   6,   7,   8,   9,   10   Extreme
pain

How are you today? Love wants to know.

_____

_____

_____

_____

_____

_____

_____

_____

_____

_____

_____

_____

_____

_____

_____

_____

#29 Date: _____

Struggling through the struggle?

Pressure creates diamonds and fire refines gold.

Are you struggling through the struggle?

_____

_____

_____

_____

_____

_____

_____

_____

_____

_____

_____

_____

_____

_____

_____

_____

_____

Date: _____

Pain Level?

No pain 0, 1, 2, 3, 4, 5, 6, 7, 8, 9, 10 Extreme
pain

How are you today? Love wants to know.

_____

_____

_____

_____

_____

_____

_____

_____

_____

_____

_____

_____

_____

#30 Date: _____

Your destiny?

I had to humble my ego to get in touch with my eagle. I humbled the me in me that was trying to keep me from my destiny. Love has given me an opportunity to share my truth with the generations that come behind me. No one will keep me from my destiny. Including me. I am I Dream Business, LLC and I Dream Business, LLC is me.

What is your destiny?

_____

_____

_____

_____

_____

_____

_____

_____

_____

_____

_____

123

Date: _____

Pain Level?

No pain　0,　1,　2,　3,　4,　5,　6,　7,　8,　9,　10　Extreme pain

How are you today? Love wants to know.

_____

_____

_____

_____

_____

_____

_____

_____

_____

_____

_____

_____

_____

_____

_____

_____

_____

_____

_____

#31 Date: _____

Who are you?

As you may remember, this was the first question asked. Don't copy what you wrote on day one. Write what you feel. Go back to the mirror. Take off all of what you feel that does not define or represent you.

Who are you?

_____

_____

_____

_____

_____

_____

_____

_____

_____

_____

_____

_____

Date: _____

Pain Level?

No pain 0, 1, 2, 3, 4, 5, 6, 7, 8, 9, 10 Extreme
pain

How are you today? Love wants to know.

_____

_____

_____

_____

_____

_____

_____

_____

_____

_____

_____

_____

_____

_____

_____

_____

_____

QUIZ FOR DRUG USE

I've included a quiz for drug use. Take this as needed.
Please stay in touch at painnorfearlivehere.com
https://drugabuse.com/library/drug-addiction-quiz/

Do you ever use drugs for something other than a medical reason?

Yes

No

When you use drugs, do you use more than one drug at a time?

Yes

No

Do you use drugs more than once per week?

Yes

No

Have you abused prescription drugs before?

Yes

No

Have you ever tried to stop using drugs but couldn't stay stopped?

Yes

No

Do you ever feel ashamed or guilty after using drugs?

Yes

No

Has your relationships with friends become distant?

Yes

No

Do you spend less time with your family and more time with drugging friends?

Yes

No

Has your family or friends talked to you about your drug use?

Yes

No

Do your family members or friends ever complain about your drug use?

Yes

No

While under the influence of drugs, have you gotten into fights with other people?

Yes

No

Have you ever lost a job due to coming in late, mistakes or poor work performance due to drug use?

Yes

No

Has your drug use caused problems or gotten you into trouble at your workplace?

Yes

No

Have you been arrested for illegal drug possession?

Yes

No

Do you participate in illegal activities in order to get your drugs?

Yes

No

When you stop taking your drug, do you experience any withdrawal symptoms or feel sick?

Yes

No

Has your drug use ever resulted in blackouts?

Yes

No

Have you ever had medical problems such as memory loss, hepatitis, convulsions, bleeding, etc. as a result of your drug use?

Yes

No

Have you ever looked for or received help for a drug problem?

Yes

No

Have you participated in any type of treatment for drug use?

Yes

No

If you answered yes to more than five of the questions on the drug addiction quiz, you may have a problem. See a professional and bring a copy of the drug addiction quiz with you or call us at **1-877-978-1577** with the answers to the drug addiction quiz. If you require help, we can find you treatment anywhere in the country. Call **1-877-978-1577.**

96579298R00074

Made in the USA
Columbia, SC
02 June 2018